WHAT DO I DO WITH THIS PAIN?

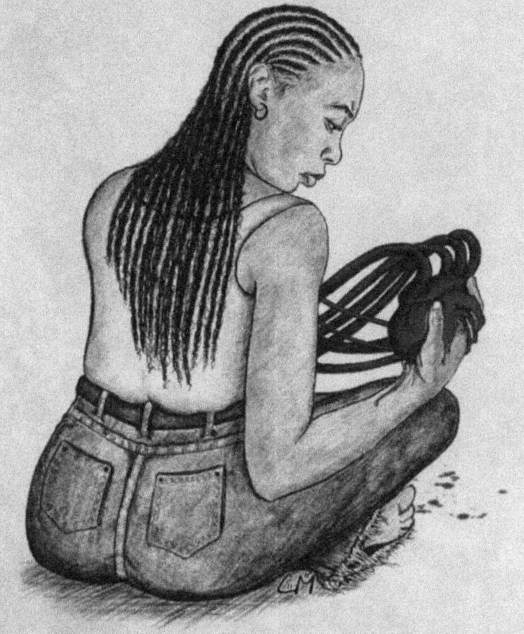

CHARISA FRANCIS

What Do I Do With This Pain?
Copyright © 2025 Charisa Francis

Published in United Kingdom
by Sekal Publishing
All rights reserved.

This book is protected under the copyright laws. This book may
not be copied or reprinted for commercial gain or profit.
The use of short quotations or occasional page copying for
personal or group study is permitted and encouraged.
Permission will be granted upon request.

Print ISBN: 978-1-7395212-8-8

All Scripture quotations are taken from the Holy Bible.

Cover Design & Illustrations by Charisa Francis
Instagram: Charisa_x

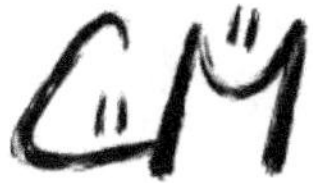

WHAT DO I DO WITH THIS PAIN?

CHARISA FRANCIS

Contents

Pain

*A feeling of physical suffering caused by injury or illness.
Emotional or mental suffering.*

[Reference: Pain definition - Cambridge Dictionary]

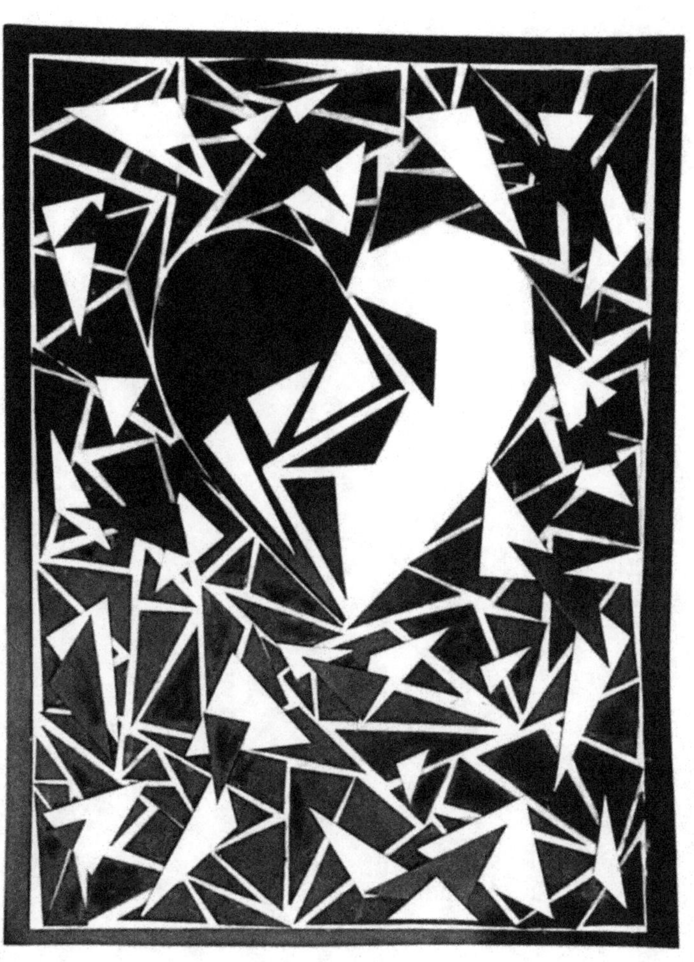

For The One Who's Searching...

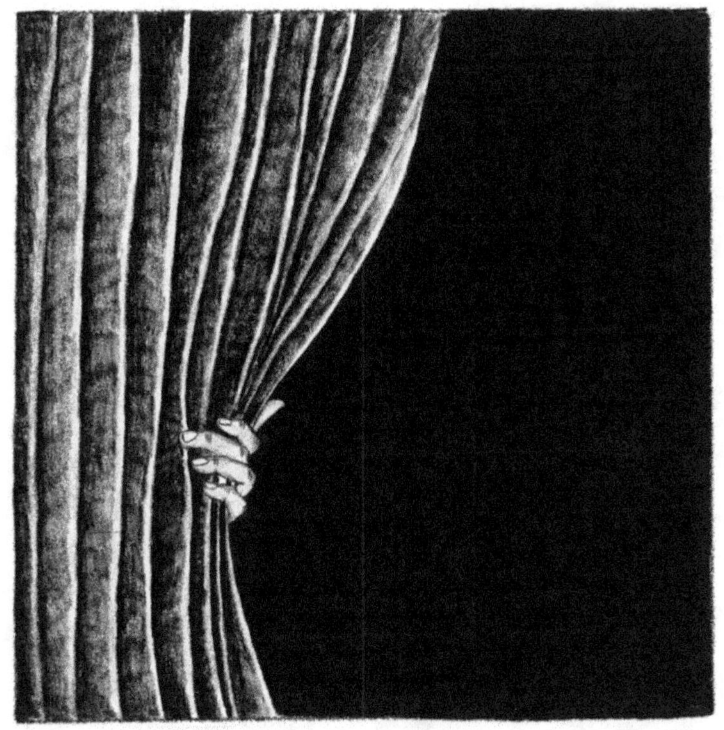

For The One Who's Searching...

I need the One whose name means the most
The great Creator of heaven and the earth
The One who orchestrates our life paths,
twists and turns
The One who knew me from before my birth

The light of the world
The epitome of glory, hope and truth
My Guide, my Protector
My Lion, My Roof

That One who saves
Who can carry us through
Our hurt, our pain
Oh Lord this pain...

For The One With Questions

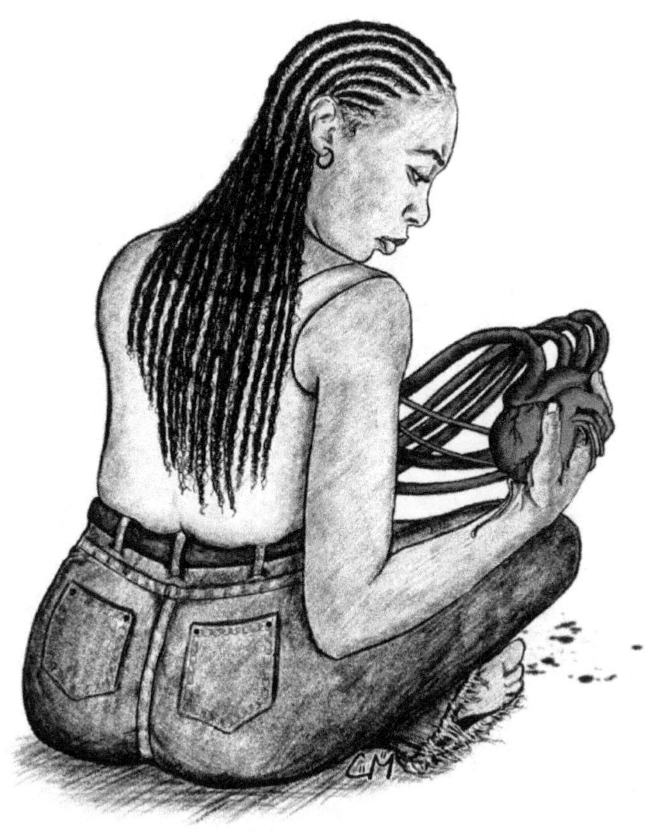

For The One With Questions...

What do I do with this pain Lord?
What do I do with this pain?
It rises up as anger inside me
Bubbling and festering
Devouring my good intentions
What do I do with this pain Lord?

It wraps itself around me in chains
Keeping me enslaved
From the inside out
Holding me back
And clothing me in doubt
What do I do with this pain Lord?

It's a hole in my soul
It's a pain in my chest
Keeping me up all night
Preventing me from rest
Making friends with stress
What do I do with this Pain Lord?

It's a high-pitched scream
A frustrated release
It's endless tears
With a bundle of fears
It's pin-drop silence
What do I do with this Pain Lord?

It's a train of thought
A nasty stain
A thousand words
A lot of blame
No words at all
What do I do with this pain Lord?

What do I do with this pain Lord?
What do I do with this pain?
I cry out, He sighs
And then my Lord replies,
"You are asking the wrong question,
Ask Me, what can I do with your pain?

A touching song
A beautiful dance
A detailed painting
That makes all stop and glance
A twenty-first century Psalm that touches hearts
That's what I'll do with your pain!

A powerful play
A candid film
A best-selling book
With a heartfelt hook
A message bringing thousands closer to Me
That's what I'll do with your pain!

A music video
A spoken word
A TV show
With respect for My word
A voice that will capture the ears of many
That's what I'll do with your pain!

An artistic vessel
An example of grace
A woman of substance
That I filled and placed

A testimony with a mouthful of praise
That's what I'll do with your Pain!"

That's what He'll do with my pain

That's what He'll do with your pain.

For The One In The Thick Of It...

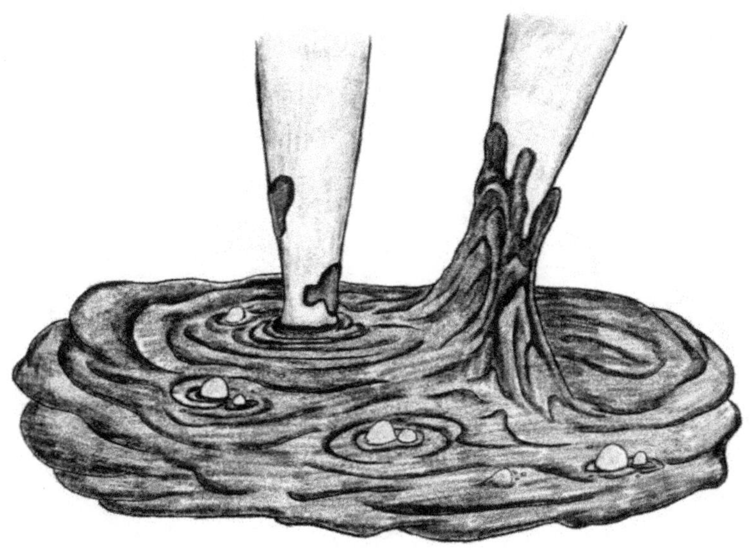

For The One In The Thick Of It...

That's what He'll do with your pain
There is purpose for you and something to gain
Although in this moment it may not feel that way
The Lord sees your pain and hears what you don't say

He's not forgotten about you
He has more for you in his depository
Although the darkness may cloud your view
This is not the end of your story.

For The One Who Encourages...

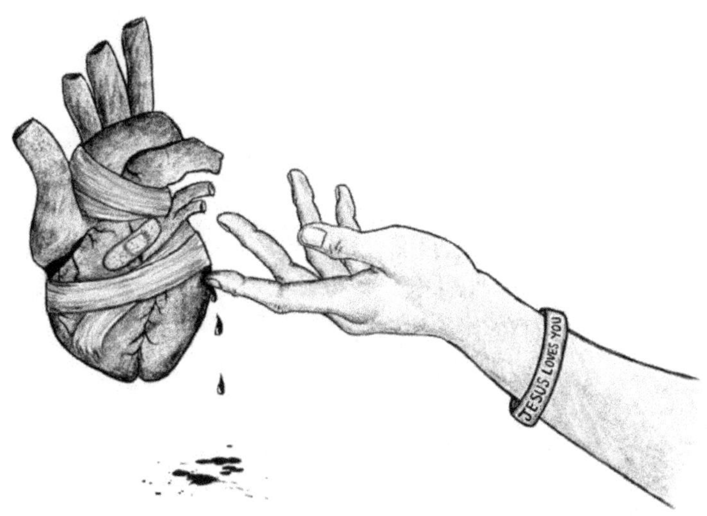

For The One Who Encourages...

When someone asks
"What do I do with this pain?"

Do you scold them and greet them with shame?
When you don't know quite what to say
Somehow we all seem to shift the blame
Trying to solve this problem we call Pain

Remember this was you once
Trying to navigate a wounded heart
Showing love to others needs wisdom in plenty
Remember Proverbs 25:20

Proverbs 25:20 (NIV)
Like one who takes away a garment on a cold day, or
like vinegar poured on a wound, is one who sings songs
to a heavy heart.

For The One Who Feels Broken...

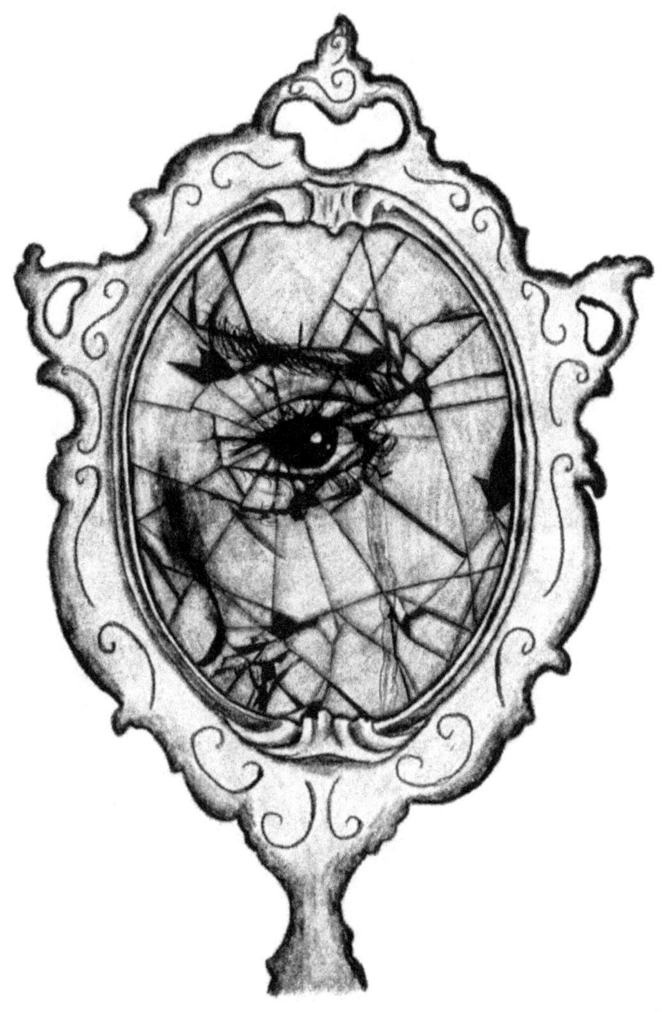

For The One Who Feels Broken...

Screwed up.
A mess.
Underdeveloped.
That's how I feel
That's what I see when I look at me

Everyone has it all wrong
They don't see all that is broken within me
Can't see the mess and distress that feels me
And weighs me down inside

It's like always seeing two versions of me
Who I was meant to be and who I became
I can't help but wish things were different
That I was different

Instead I'm screwed up.
A mess.
Underdeveloped.
That's how I feel
That's what I see when I look at me

I spent all my time and energy
Trying to mend and repair
Broken and missing pieces of me
But it's as if some things can't be fixed or found

Tell me, please tell me
How does a hiker keep going with broken limbs?
Whilst missing vital hiking gear
How can they possibly climb, or run or jump?

They can't and neither can I
Because I'm screwed up
A mess
Underdeveloped
That's how I feel
And that's what I see when I look at me

That's what I see when I look at me
I sigh, I cry
And then a Still Small Voice replies,
"Your vision is off, Open your eyes
Ask Me, what I see when I look at you?

Strength is made perfect
In your weakness
I fill in the gaps
I mend all the pieces

In the womb I knew you
I spent time creating you
You are My child
Created in My image
I'm not changing you for someone else
You are just what I wanted
Unique and special just as I intended

Raised up.
A gift.
Underdevelopment.
Love is how I feel
And that's what I see when I look at you."

For The One Who Is Rejected...

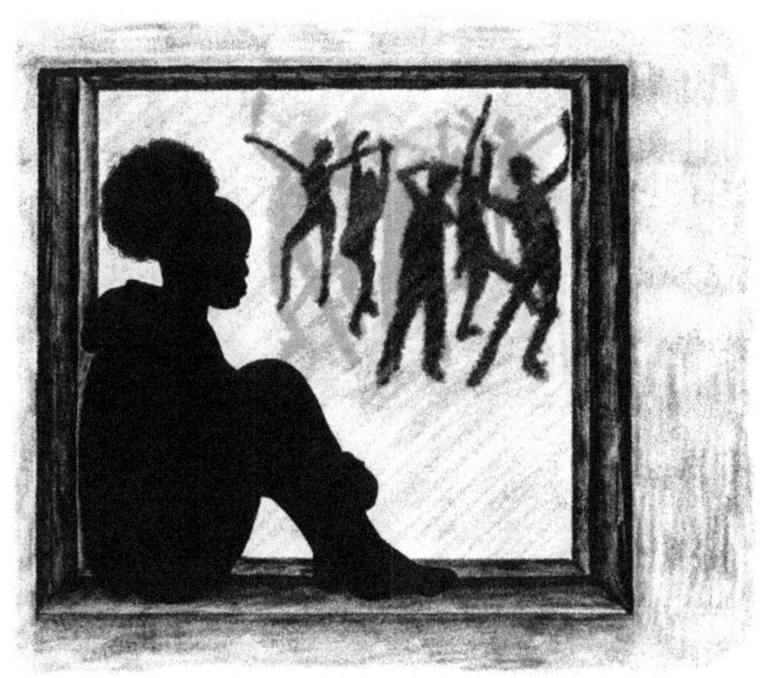

For The One Who Is Rejected...

The pain of being rejected
When you're the one that's just not selected
Somehow while you're trying to keep everyone
included
You find yourself the one excluded
Like access denied
It's a deep loneliness inside
A growing distance you try to close
But no matter what you propose
The avoidance shows
And that pain inside grows

Take it on the chin, sing a fitting song
But they all seem to fit, they all seem to belong
One of Maslow's needs in your heart
Asking "Why can't I be a part?"

So you try to be useful
You show up and keep it cool
You go out of your way
Trying to eliminate any excuse they may say

But you still find yourself slighted
You're still uninvited
Wondering what did you do wrong?
To not fit, to not belong

"Why not me?
Why can't it be me?
Why don't they pick me?
Why don't they want me—
Around?
Am I too loud?
Do I not make enough of a sound?"
Second guessing
So depressing

But hold on, take a beat, wait
Let me give you another take
Take heart
Don't confuse rejection with being set apart
You are to be in this world but not a part
Understanding this is the start
You can tarry
But some just can't handle what you carry

So yes, you may not be the one people choose
On the outside looking in, missing social cues
Overlooked, Misunderstood, at the back of the queue
But God loves you and He already chose you.

For The One Who Feels Weak...

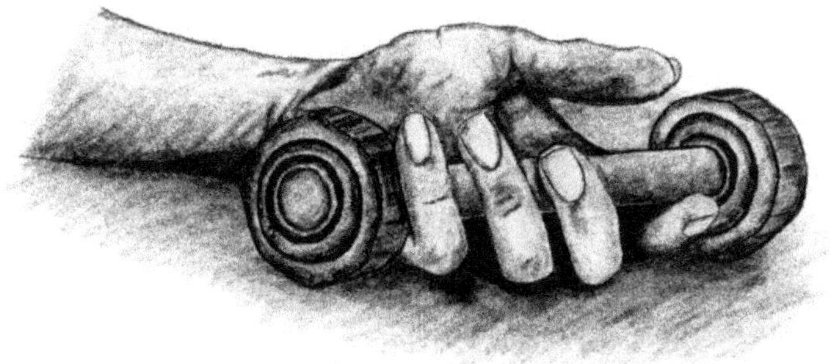

For The One Who Feels Weak...

Your weapon is your strength
Don't you know?
Your ability to withstand the storms and attacks
When knives and swords pierce your skin
Your skin bounces back
Stronger
Tougher
With an extra layer
Real life superheroes
Don't you see you're impenetrable?
They continue to throw jabs and stabs
But they can't keep you down
So they attack your mind
They make you think you're weak
And you can't get up
But they've already lost
Because you're impenetrable
They know that
And you should too
Your weapon is your strength
Because every time you get up and keep going
They get weaker

They're fighting a losing battle
They know it
And it's draining them
But you keep getting stronger
Like Wolverine
Your skin is thick
And soon their blades won't even be able to make a
dent
Because your weapon is your strength
And your strength comes from God
Don't you know?

For The One With Regrets...

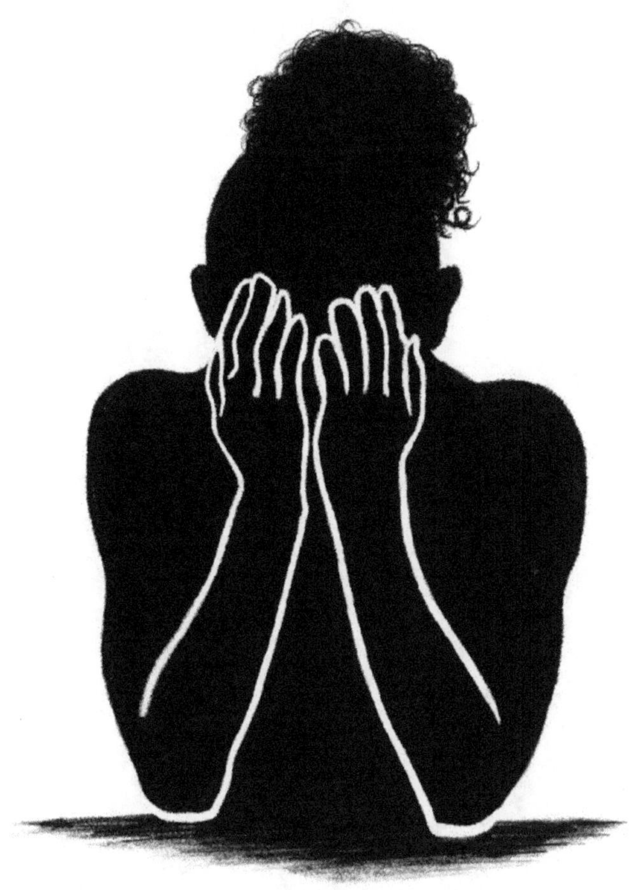

For The One With Regrets...

Stop counting the time wasted
When you have a future you have not yet tasted
It's about time you even the score
Because every step and misstep has been accounted for
With purpose too great for you to comprehend
and foresee
Guiding you to your now, exactly where you're
meant to be

So give yourself a break
From rehearsing the pain and torturing yourself,
for goodness sake!
Tell your thoughts to be kind
God is not a man that he would lie or change His mind
About you, with all you have been through
And whatever you feel has disqualified you

Don't let your yesterday stain today
Mistakes made then is what will show you the way
Forgive yourself, it is time to move on
There's greater things for you to experience, meditate
and look upon.

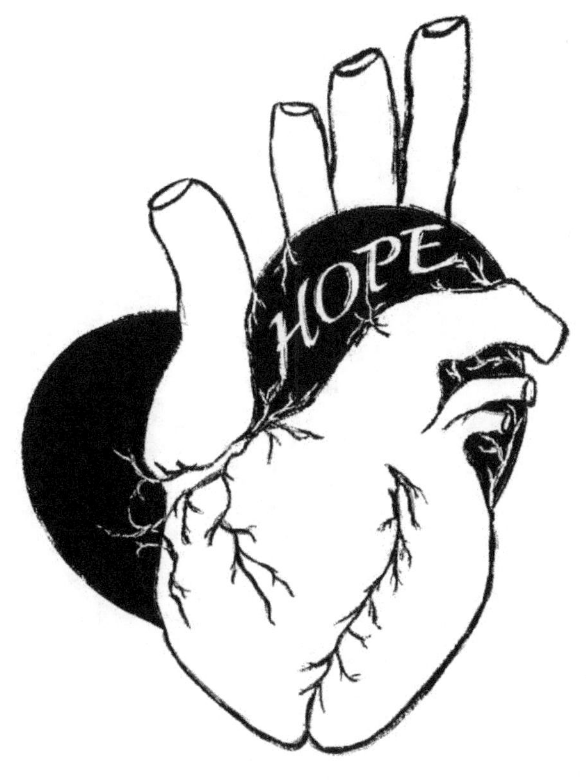

Jeremiah 29:11 (NLT)
For I know the plans I have for you," says the Lord.
"They are plans for good and not for disaster,
to give you a future and a hope.